Saltwater
AND
Silence

ELISSAR MUSTAPHA

Ordering Information:

Prime Seven Media
518 Landmann St.
Tomah City, WI 54660

Printed in the United States of America

Table of Contents

broken porcelain

i think about smashing plates
but then again, i don't.
there's a certain weight in porcelain,
in the idea of fracture,
but i hold still,
perfect in my stillness.
the eldest curse, or maybe just a design flaw,
a crack in the mould that no one talks about.
they said i was meant to hold things together,
but somewhere along the line,
something slipped.
or maybe nothing ever held at all.
was there a beginning?
a moment of break?
or have i always been
a slow collapse,
splintering quietly while the world keeps asking,
"what happened?"
as if the answer matters.

Elissar Mustapha

starfall

stars falling
from down here,
it's all glitter and grace,
soft streaks of light,
like promises no one asked for,
whispers we can't quite catch.
we call it beauty
because it slips through our fingers—
something rare,
or maybe something lost.
the sky doesn't answer,
it just lets the stars fall,
and we watch,
pretending to understand.
but what is it, really?
a flicker before it fades,
a moment we try to hold
as it crumbles.
maybe it's love,
or maybe just time—
burning up, falling apart,
until there's nothing left
but the quiet.
from up there,
it's hard to tell if the light means anything,
or if it ever did.
but we look anyway,
hoping the pieces that break
will somehow fill the spaces
we didn't know were empty.

The Quiet Flame

i never thought i'd watch the world
like a stranger,
but here i am—
eyes tracing the movement of shadows
that slip by,
hands in pockets,
unseen.

it's strange to wonder
if feeling ordinary is the most extraordinary thing of all.
people drift alone, together, apart.
they say life hums beneath it all,
but sometimes the silence
says more than any heart could.

i'm just one in a thousand—
a face in the blur,
neither here nor gone,
no ripple in the surface
when i walk through the room.
i tried to be a spark once,
tried to be loud enough for the stars to hear,
but maybe they weren't listening,
or maybe i wasn't burning right.

there's a soft ache in watching from the outside,
seeing the birds in pairs,
the lights that flicker for someone else.
maybe i was meant for the margins,

to lift others like wind beneath wings,
while my own stay heavy with the weight of quiet.
perhaps my purpose is to be the invisible thread,
holding everything together,
yet never seen,
never unravelling into my own.

but i want to be known—
to be more than whispers caught in the breeze,
more than just
the space between someone else's brilliance.
i don't want the mundane,
not the slow churn of days that leave no mark,
but something that lingers
long after the last breath.

and still, i drift.
like a feather in a wind
that doesn't know its destination,
like a question without an answer,
floating,
always floating.
i think i had roots once—
a place to stand—
but now i'm only the echo of a beginning
that got lost in the swirl.

people say there's beauty in simplicity,
that life is in the small things,
the unnoticed,
the forgotten.

ow do you make peace with fading
en you want to burn so brightly
the sky remembers your name?

i'm tired of watching.
the birds, the crowds,
the faces i'll never meet.
the truth is, i feel like a ghost
in a world that's too alive,
a quiet figure haunting corners
while the rest soar.

maybe i was meant to bear
the weight of others' dreams,
to be the pillar beneath them all
as they rise.
maybe this is who i am—
the one who stays behind,
the one who watches.

but how do you make peace with that?
how do you watch yourself sink
while the shore is still in view?
there's something in me that won't give in—
a flame that refuses to die,
even when it should.

i feel selfish for wanting more,
but sometimes,
the world feels cruel for giving less.
and i wonder—

is it selfish to want to be seen,
or is it the quietest form of longing?
maybe i'm both—
a feather,
and the wind that carries it.

and yet,
despite it all,
i stand in a life that isn't mine,
with a heart that feels too full of nothing
to ever understand why.
there are no words for this,
just a quiet storm.

perhaps,
in the end,
i will learn myself,
not as the shadow in someone else's light,
but as the flame
that was always there—
waiting
to be seen.

No Mercy?

no mercy?
no *mercy*?
how can you say that,
when we've weathered storms
no one else could see,
and still—
still,
we stayed?
how can you call it heartless
when the only thing keeping me here
is the ache in my chest
that bends, breaks, and folds
just to keep you warm?
no mercy,
when all my thoughts orbit you—
every step,
every breath,
a quiet offering?
how can you forget the weight i carry,
the way i've been crushed beneath it,
mowed down
again and again,
yet somehow, i rise
just to keep this going?
no mercy—
when all i wanted was your happiness,
when all i gave
was the last piece of me
that hadn't yet shattered.
no damn mercy?

Between The Gaze

why do your eyes linger on me,
a silent storm behind the glass?
i can't trace the shape of your gaze—
is it accusation, or something unspoken?
am i a shadow you wish to forget,
or a reflection you can't quite hold?
tell me, do you even see me at all,
or am i just the space between your thoughts?

Elissar Mustapha

why do your eyes linger on me,
a silent storm behind the glass?

Surface.

stick your stickers on a sticky surface

make sure it cannot come off

be honest about why you do this

does it make you feel better when your leg shakes?

or is it why your leg shakes?

Saltwater and Silence

stick your stickers on a sticky surface

make sure it cannot come off

be honest about why you do this

Circles of the Past

a carousel of forgotten wishes,
spinning on the edge of childhood dreams—
why did we cling so tightly,
to that dizzying blur of light and sound?
perhaps it was the fleeting weightlessness,
the feeling of flying without wings,
as the world melted into soft hues,
and time became nothing but a circle,
endlessly turning,
lifting us from the ground,
only to return us,
changed, but never quite knowing how.
in that fleeting motion,
we found a moment of release,
a breath between the noise,
and for a heartbeat,
we were infinite.

Ode to a Student

am i writing this to procrastinate,
or perhaps i am finally finding time to ruminate?
perhaps a bit of both.
maybe i am simply just doing a finger warm up.
i don't really want to tackle this essay,
nobody ever does—
but what's the other option?
ponder, weigh, assess;
speculate all the decisions i've made in my life
all the missed opportunities.
missed people. missed memories.
missed apologies? mistakes?
i am just writing this to procrastinate.

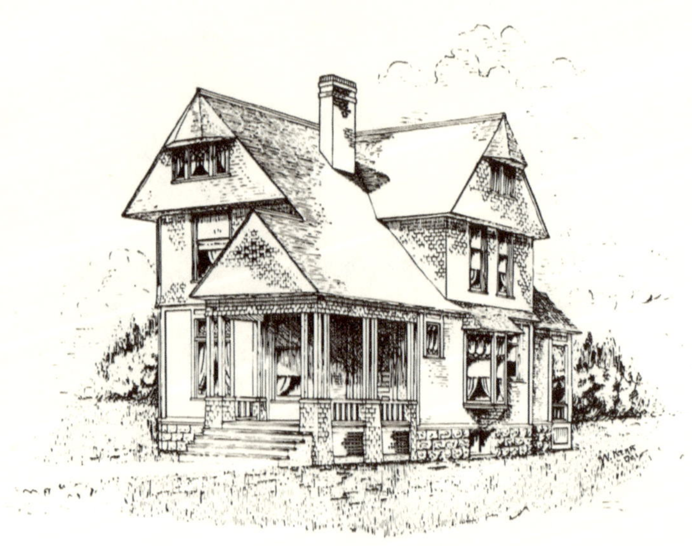

Engulfed by Surrender

it is mine,

all of it,

a quiet surrender,

a softness in the way i gave.

i stood still,

too timid to resist,

too fragile to fight.

i allowed the shadows to wrap me,

allowed them to shape me

until i became the echo of my own collapse—

a fall i made with trembling hands,

a descent i chose without knowing it.

unspoken

the question lingers,
a quiet ache—
when will i ever be enough?
i long to live in the space of my own breath,
untethered, unclaimed,
to need no one,
to need nothing but the weight of my own skin.
i wish i could exist in that simplicity,
untouched by the pull of you,
untangled from the threads of love that tie me.

want—
such a tender thing,
woven into the fabric of our human pulse.
but with each thread,
guilt seeps through the seams,
like an uninvited guest
who arrives without warning,
without mercy.
why must want carry the weight of shame,
like a shadow that never fades?

D-S-O-N-C-

connect through the disconnection,
what else is there left to say?
what lies ahead is imperfection
don't tell me i've doomed the day.

Conscience

this burden has become my skin,
woven into the marrow of my bones,
a weight that never lifts,
a pressure that never wanes.

mould

i don't know why you keep pulling me apart,
like some cruel game that only you understand.
it feels as though you find joy in my unravelling,
like each tug of your hands feeds something dark in you.
i am not your toy,
your fragile little doll to dress and discard
when your hands grow tired of my shape,
when i no longer fit the image you wanted.

you cannot lock me away,
hidden in the cold, forgotten corners,
where only shadows are allowed to see me.
i am meant to move, to breathe, to *live*.
i want to stretch beyond these walls,
to see the light, to feel the pulse of the world
beneath my feet.

i deserve more than this cage,
more than this silence.
i cannot go on like this,
not trapped in a story where i never get to speak.

Elissar Mastapha

Echoes of a Dying Wish

i will never be free,

so long as my heart still beats.

forever i will bow beneath

the unseen weight of this phantom hand,

its touch like iron on my bones,

its shadow stitched into my skin.

this part of me—

this echo of something i never asked for—

must vanish,

dissolve like mist before the dawn.

i cannot exist in this hollow,

this trembling shell of what i was.

i wish it would unravel,

fall away like dust in the wind,

and leave me—

empty,

and free.

Elissar Mastapha

Broken Shell

am i destined to become you?
to wear your skin,
to walk the path you've paved,
where duty and work swallow every breath,
and joy is a foreign language?
is this what you're preparing me for—
to be nothing but a reflection,
a shadow of your unyielding grip,
a life where fun is a sin
and rest is a luxury you never allowed?

i am not you,
i do not want this life,
this endless cycle of sacrifice for the sake of nothing.
is this what you're "protecting" me from?
a life beyond your reach,
a life that doesn't mirror your misery?

you will carve every piece of me out,
slowly, meticulously,
until i am nothing but a hollow shell—
ready to be filled with your idea of what i should be.
But i don't want your life,
not this cage,
not this silence.

please,
set me free.

Broken Puzzle Piece

tried, i have—
countless times,
but with hands that tremble,
i cannot piece together
what was never meant to align.
all the wrong fragments,
sharp and uneven,
no matter how i force them,
they remain broken,
a shattered reflection of what could have been.

perhaps in time,
i'll learn—
some souls,
no matter how deeply we reach,
will never find their way into each other,
always drifting
on the edges of what could have been.

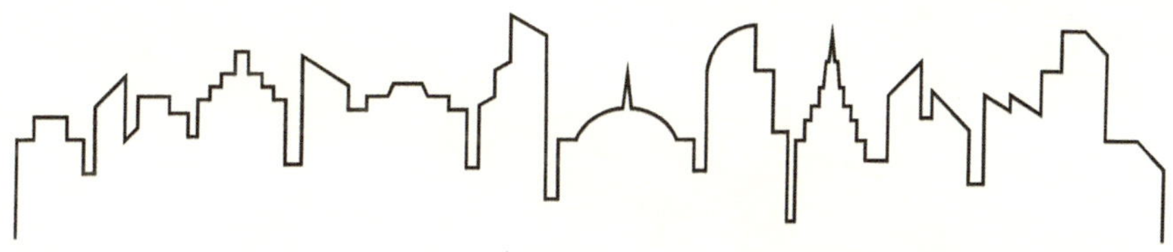

Love Behind Glass

the art is hiding behind
one pretence or another,
for surely it cannot be both of these?
hidden things cannot stay hidden,
for found is where beauty is.

hate.
the incessant whining of an ache
behind my ear,
and it is like the wind whistling
between glass at an ungodly hour.
like smoke between teeth.

the world does not obey your thoughts,
does not listen to my wishes.
so tell me your name,
at least one time,
tell me your name
so that i may place it in my mind,
in a place where it can live
and dance and rot and forever remain,
and let me say, "i love you."

love doesn't exist.
it is the chemicals
that are held in the heavy weight
of your tears.

Find the Beauty

simple things are the most beautiful,
but to find beauty in simplicity,
you must fall in love with the mundane,
with ordinary life.

falling in love with a soul is anything but simple,
yet it is the simple things that make falling in love easier:
a beautiful word, carelessly mentioned,
the shape of one's heart, visible through their eyes—
your eyes.
hands and collarbones,
simple things that another may not even notice,
you may never even guess.

but every small, mundane thing adds up,
and creates something larger than you could ever imagine.

x_X

simplicity isn't always beauty,
for sometimes it translates
into something shallow,
a mask for ignorance—
obnoxious words spilling
from an uneducated mouth,
loud but empty,
too eager to be heard,
too blind to listen.

روحي

death will tap your shoulder
seven times a lifetime
that's what i've learnt
but when you whip your head around
death will have been long gone
and i suppose it's fun to think about
that maybe death came and stood behind me for an
entire week
but that's not how death works
death will come to greet you at even intervals
perhaps once when you are fourteen
and again when you are twenty one
and then when you are thirty nine

i am twenty now
and death scares me just as much as when i was a child
not the thought of dying,
but the thought of leaving things unfinished.

Sway

i think people don't ever understand what i mean
he hands her his cigarette
as if in wordless consolation
she does not smoke
and she has never touched a cigarette until this moment
she meets his extended hand half way
she wraps her fingers around the instrument
as if it were a crutch
your cigarette anchors you
she tells him, but does not think he understands
he anchors her
anchor on rocky bay
the world around them is the wind
and she is the boat
mercilessly, harshly rocked
on the water's surface
until she is hitting the rocky shore
over and over
over and over
hurting
just to stay anchored to him
i wish you understood.

You Amongst Stars

the stars remind me of things
they will never remind you of.
you will look at them
and see only what they are—
silent, distant,
unchanging.
but when I look,
i see you.

i will always look up at the stars,
hoping,
just hoping,
that you are looking too.
but in their light,
i find you—
your name traced in constellations,
your voice whispered in the spaces between.

i read the stars like braille,
fingertips brushing across memories,
each one telling the story of us—
the one we wrote together,
the one i carry,
the one that stays
even when you don't.

Qamar

the moon is shy,
she hides herself away,
always veiled,
partly cloaked in darkness.
but in the quiet moments,
when the world is still,
when the air hums with the right energy—
you see her,
soft and radiant,
in all her glowing glory.

Fire Would

warmth

a fire that needs kindling

it's dying out

we've lost the tinder stick

so i blow

i fill up my lungs until they hurt

inhale

exhale

my head spins and there is no air

i do it again

i don't save any for myself

i am dizzy

the ash is swirling

up in the air

inhale

exhale

my chest is going to burst

the ash is settling on my skin

tattooing the harsh reminder

of how much i give

inhale

exhale

i can no longer see

inhale. exhale.

i have done all that i can

all that remains is my soul

my heart has abandoned me

my lungs have died

my mind is on the outs with me,
she says i shouldn't even try
do i throw it into the embers, too?
perhaps that's all it needs to stay alight forever
but i am too tired now
i never listen

Whiplash

you drag me through midnights,
pressing sweet nothings into my skin
only to turn brittle by morning.
i fold myself into the silence you leave behind,
wondering if love should feel like this—
like a hand reaching, only to recoil.
three weeks and i've drowned in saltwater,
held together by the weight of my own care.
too much, too soon, too soft—
but never enough to keep you steady.
i should leave before the waves pull me under,
before i forget what air feels like.
homesickness twists itself into my bones,
but i am not longing for places,
only for something that feels like warmth,
something that does not vanish
when i reach for it.
i am stretched between two worlds,
and you, you make neither feel like home.
isn't love supposed to be easier?
or did i misread the signs,
mistake illusion for devotion,
soft-spoken lies for longing?
i am not wrong.
i am flesh and soul and poetry,
and you—
you are a shadow i mistook for light.
i try to write,

but my hands are empty.
you have stolen the words
and left me with echoes of promises
never meant to be kept.
and yet, still,
i sit in the ruins of our almost,
cradling the hurt like an old friend,
pretending i do not feel the fracture,
pretending i do not break that way.

Indiscernible

i don't know what to do,
only that i am ruined by you.
only that you slip through me like water,
like smoke,
like something i was never meant to hold.

i call it love because i have no other name for it,
no other way to explain the ache in my chest,
the way my body flinches at the absence of your voice.
but love should not feel like translating silence,
should not feel like swallowing glass just to speak.

i dreamt you lost your mind,
ripped the walls apart with your hands,
screamed so loud the sky shattered—
but maybe it was only a reflection,
maybe i was the one unraveling,
thread by thread,
whisper by whisper,
until i no longer recognised my own outline.

they say you are like an old friend,
but nostalgia is a liar,
wrapping ghosts in familiar warmth,
making graves feel like home.

a name blurred beyond recognition,
a voice that echoes but never stays.
you laugh, and it sounds like a bird in freefall,
like a warning, like a dirge.

the night folds around me,
a hand over my mouth,
a knife to my ribs,
and i am still waiting for an answer
that i am too afraid to ask for.

my hands are tired,
cupped around a flickering light,
as if i can force it to stay,
as if it will not die in the end.

expectations.
salutations.
i bend at the weight of it all.

And Still, I Stay

i spit out my teeth in the dark,
count the losses like pearls in my palm,
but you tell me to smile,
tell me it isn't that bad,
tell me i bruise so beautifully.

i have always been *not okay,*
but you like me better that way—
soft-spoken, soft-spined,
a thing that folds, a thing that stays.
you love me in halves,
in rationed affection,
in punishments i do not deserve.

you *stay up for me*
and i mistake it for devotion,
even when the sun comes up
and i am nothing but an afterthought,
even when your voice sharpens at dawn,
even when love sounds more like a warning.

i wake up to silence,
to rooms colder than i left them,
to the ghost of your warmth
on the other side of the bed.

you have made me a body that apologises,
a mouth that swallows its own hunger,
a heart that keeps beating despite itself.

is this love?
is this sacrifice?
is there a difference?

i have always felt too much,
but you don't feel at all—
not when i cry, not when i break,
not when i look at you and wonder
if you have ever really seen me.

i loved you like i loved coffee,
pretending to enjoy the bitterness,
convincing myself it made me strong,
but the truth is, it made me sick—
it *has always made me sick.*

and still, i stay.

Elissar Mustapha

The Opposite of Indifference

i want you—
and i don't even know why.
once, your name was something i spat out,
something bitter at the back of my throat.
now, it lingers like a prayer
i can't bring myself to stop saying.

how did i come to love
what i once despised?
maybe love and loathing
are the same beast,
writhing in the same dark,
a two-headed creature gnawing at my ribs.
perhaps indifference would have saved me.
perhaps it would have killed me slower.

you never promised me anything,
but still, I sit here,
pulling at the loose threads
of a future you never wove for me.

I don't even know if you are mine to love,
but the thought of another's hands on your skin
claws at my stomach like sickness.
And still, I cannot see myself—
not without you,
not beyond you,
not past this ruinous ache
you will never even feel.

I Wish It Were Otherwise

I just want to see you again
talk to your face
figure it all out
maybe it's wishful thinking

I just want to see you again—
pull you from the static of my mind,
watch your mouth shape words
instead of reading them in silence.

I want to trace the lines of your face,
search for answers in the way you look at me,
hold time between my hands
like something I could control.

Maybe then I'd understand.
Maybe then I'd know what this is,
if it is anything at all.

Or maybe it's just wishful thinking—
a fever dream I refuse to wake from.

Breathless

I think I loved you before I knew your name.
Or maybe I just loved the way you looked at me—
like I was something soft, something worth keeping.

I don't know if you love me,
but I know I make you feel something.
I know I live in the corners of your mind,
where the light doesn't reach.

You hold me at arm's length
but keep me close enough to watch me ache.
I think you like watching me ache.
I think you love the way I need you.
I think you love being needed more than you love me.

You push, I pull, we break, we mend,
but I don't know how many times
I can put myself back together.
Maybe one day I'll stop trying.

Maybe one day, you'll notice.
Maybe that will be the day you decide to stay.
Maybe that will be the day I don't want you to.

No Exit

I love you. God, I wish I didn't.
I wish you were cruel enough to make it easy,
but you hurt me just softly enough to keep me.
I don't think you love me.
Maybe you don't know how.
Maybe you just don't want to.

I tell myself it's not a choice,
that maybe you are incapable,
that maybe your hands were never taught
to hold without breaking—
but how many times can I pretend
the shards in my chest aren't yours?

I know I should leave.
I know I should let go.
But I am caught in the space between knowing and doing,
between drowning and breathing,
and you are the tide that never recedes.

How long before I let the water take me?

Pyrolysis

You are all heat and ruin,
anger wrapped in the shape of a man,
yet somehow, you are my calm.
The irony does not slip past me—
the wildfire and the girl made of paper,
the way she lets herself curl at the edges,
blacken, crack, smolder—
if only it means he will stay.

She doesn't need him to.
She just learned that love is warm,
and she has been cold for so long.
So maybe the fact that he burns—
maybe that means he loves her.
That's not wrong, is it?

I am burning.
I may burn brighter before I die,
but dying stars are beautiful, aren't they?
I am suffocating.
But in your arms, I swear—
for just a moment—
I have never been more alive.

Fading Map

I wish I knew if I'll be okay—
but the lines of where I'm meant to go
keep bleeding into something else.
Everything feels like it's been erased
before it was ever written down.
I watch others move in their straight lines,
like they've been handed a map
and told to follow the paths,
while I'm left tracing shadows
on a page that doesn't make sense anymore.
It's not about where they're headed.
It's the way they don't question the direction.
They don't feel the earth shifting
underneath their feet,
like the ground is tired of holding them.
What if I don't need to find a way?
What if there's something in the waiting
I'm supposed to break open?
Or is it just a matter of running in circles
until I forget what it means to move forward?
Maybe this pause isn't an accident,
but a place I've been trying to outrun.
I don't know if I'm meant to catch up
or if I'll just keep falling
into spaces I never understood.

Ashes of Who I Was

There's a version of me
that used to burn bright.
She flickered,
without hesitation,
without asking for permission.
She knew what it was
to be alive—
and now I'm left wondering
if I was ever her at all.

The fire didn't die in a single breath,
no.
It was smothered
slowly,
like something that was never meant to be touched.
I don't know when I stopped feeling
the warmth in my chest.
I just know I'm empty now,
and no one warned me
how it would feel
to forget
who I was.

I can't find her.
She's somewhere behind these walls,
built of silence,
of words I never said,
of things I never let myself feel.

I think she's still there,
but every time I reach out,
my fingers just pass through the dust.

I've learned how to smile,
but it's a smile that cracks when it gets too close to
the surface.
I don't know who I'm pretending for anymore—
or if pretending even matters.
I used to think love could heal me.
I thought it could burn through all the rust
and bring the sparks back.
But all it did was turn me into a shadow,
and now
I'm afraid
of the dark I've become.

Sometimes,
I wonder if I was always meant to burn
only to become ash.
And maybe
that's all I'll ever be now—
a pile of things I couldn't let go of,
caught between what I was
and what I could have been.

The Silence Left Behind

Your death was expected,
a shadow long before the fall,
creeping,
quiet,
the kind of ending
no one has the courage
to speak aloud.
Still,
you took with you
the best of us—
the light that never made it
past the door,
the laugh that wasn't allowed
to echo,
the love we couldn't
reach in time.

And now we stand
in the silence you left behind,
like ghosts haunted by their own names.
We wait for answers
that will never come,
for a moment we never
asked for,
for a finality
that feels like a wound
that won't stop bleeding.

Did you know
when you left
you stole more than you gave?
You took the pieces
of us that believed in you,
and we're left here,
clutching at things
that have already slipped through
our fingers.

Hurt is Subjective

Hurt doesn't have a name
or a face,
it's the space between
what was said
and what was meant.
It's in the things
that never made it out
of my throat,
swallowed down like glass.

Elissar Mustapha

Misplaced Summertime

Maybe loving you is my punishment—
what it's meant to teach me, I don't know,
but I'll find out eventually.
Everyone has their regrets,
but I wonder,
does mine deserve this?

I stay here, in the place we were—
This past July,
when the air was thick and our skin was damp,
and the stars spun
like they knew something we didn't.
I watched them
and you watched me,
like I was worth something.
In that misplaced summer,
I couldn't tell where you ended
and I began,
where we melted into each other
without needing to say a word.
We were one.
Beginning and ending, all at once.

I miss us—
this past June,
when your tenderness came easy,
as if it was me
bleeding into you,
as if you could feel me in your bones.

I miss the way your touch was calm,
the way your gaze softened,
like you knew something I didn't
but for once,
you understood me.

Threshold of Small Things

Beneath a low hum,
something lingers between the teeth of silence.
It waits, edges soft but unbroken,
in the spaces where metal sighs,
where the night sips at itself
in slow drags.

Time pools in corners,
thick as forgotten words,
half-open, half-swallowed.
There are offerings here—
delicate, plain as a whisper,
held in the faint light of maybe.

You sit with your quiet gods,
and the world stays suspended
on the rim of the smallest hunger,
as if nothing,
as if everything
could break open
at any moment.

Elissar Mustapha

What Passes Between

There's a warmth that hovers,
not quite here, not quite there—
an exhale left unfinished,
cradling the weight of something too small to
name.

Outside, the air bends,
pulled taut by a rhythm
that touches everything but leaves no mark.
A steady pulse, an endless return
to a place it never began.

Inside, things move slower—
each breath a gesture,
each pause a reflection
of a world blurred at the edges.
Everything settles for a moment
in the quiet of almost,
of never-quite-said.

You sit with it, feeling the weight shift,
knowing it's all slipping through
but holding on anyway,
as if this moment between could linger
a little longer
before it fades
into the next.

The Secret Tension of Things

A quiet ritual stirs,
its breath caught on the lip of time,
ribbons of heat unspool from an unseen source,
twisting into shapes the eye refuses.
Something swells,
a pulse, a flare—
small violences contained within glass and waiting.

Outside, a sky shatters softly,
fractures spill down, chasing their own echoes.
Each drop, a reckless messenger,
falls with the certainty of forgetting.
The earth opens itself wide,
a lover to this undoing,
this restless, quenching fury.

And still, inside the moment,
the air holds itself taut—
something is on the verge of breaking
or becoming,
its arrival too grand for silence,
its departure too light for memory.

You stay here, suspended in this sharp inhale,
where what isn't seen cracks open the world,
where every quiet is the verge of a storm
and every storm carries the weight
of something hot
and brimming
just beneath your hands.

Elissar Mustapha

The Space Between Threads

She moves slowly, like gravity presses harder here,
her fingers pulling at the unseen,
drawing threads from air itself—
delicate and trembling,
each one a whisper of something already lost.
Her hands are skilled,
but there's a softness to the way they falter,
as though she's weaving not to create
but to keep from unravelling.

Beside her, something watches.
Green eyes flicker like distant stars
in the black quiet.
There's a knowing in their gaze,
but it's too old, too deep for her to reach.
The silence between them pulses,
the weight of everything unsaid,
everything held just beneath the surface.

She pulls the strands tighter—
tighter, but never tight enough.
It slips, always slips,
through her hands, through the cracks in her thoughts.
The more she weaves, the more it frays,
the more she feels the hollow tug
of something that isn't hers to keep.

Far away—

too far to touch but close enough to hurt,

a shadow pulls at her.

It's not here, but it lives in her hands,

in the trembling threads she tries to control.

He lingers there,

a name that can't be spoken,

a wound she can't forget,

distance thick with his absence,

and somehow heavier than his presence ever was.

The cat shifts beside her,

its eyes glinting with a truth

she doesn't want to know.

They see how the strings pull at her wrists,

how they tighten,

how they lead somewhere she cannot follow.

The loom keeps moving,

her hands keep moving—

but the shape of the weave is not hers,

and it never was.

She wants to scream, but all that comes

is the soft rhythm of thread passing through thread,

of time passing through her hands,

of love passing through pain

until all of it feels the same.

Devotion as Self-Destruction

Why can't you see—
your hands are knives
and I am made of wax?

I pour and pour,
an ocean emptying itself into your cupped palms,
but you only drink when you're thirsty.

My brain softens, a fruit left too long in the sun,
my heart erupts, a star swallowing itself whole.
Still, you say nothing.
Your silence crawls beneath my skin,
a parasite feasting on the spaces where joy used to live.

You dim me like a dying bulb,
pulling the cord just before the light can settle.
And yet, you think I have no right to flicker.
No right to shatter under the weight of my own erasure.

I exist when your sky is clear,
but when your storms roll in, I vanish—
a silhouette smudged from the page.
Your love is a breath held too long,
only exhaled when it suits you.

You tell me I am your world.
Lies have never dripped so sweet,
never burned so deeply
until they fell from your lips.

I hate what you carve me into,
but not more than I hate
how willingly I hand you the blade.

Trophy Wings

I fell, not from grace,
but from the wreckage of you.

Once, I was untouchable—
a thing of light, of air, of gold-threaded quiet.
And then you laid your hands on me,
stained me like an afterthought,
like another ghost passing through your ruin.

I became just another body,
another name to be left unsaid,
another monument to your undoing.

You clipped my wings and strung them up,
trophies rattling in the wind,
proof of what you can take and still remain empty.

You made me love you.
And I let you.
Easily.

If you had taken my sight,
I would have sworn you led me somewhere safe.
Even as you fed your own hunger first,
even as you left my ribs hollow.
And yet you call *me* selfish?
Ha.

You are a man orbiting only himself,
a centrepoint of need,
and still, I tried to hold you steady,
tried to keep you from vanishing into yourself.

And you—
you met my hands with iron spiked ones,
made a home of my bleeding heart
then told me not to flinch.

Tender as Ruin

I am nothing to you but softness—
soft skin beneath careless hands,
soft heart bent into your shape,
soft words swallowed by your storm,
soft tears sinking into the soil.

You have planted me in sorrow,
pressed my weeping into a punnet of mulch,
whispered grow, grow
until my grief took root,
until it split the earth,
twisting upward into a tree of hurt,
of melancholy,
of pain.

And still, you stand beneath its branches,
hands outstretched,
waiting for the fruit.

"Man Enough"

I bring you gifts wrapped in ribbons you'll gladly unwrap,
write you letters full of words I'll never hear back,
pour my heart into your hands
as if you could hold it—
but you just let it slip,
like it's nothing.

I have learned how to shrink,
how to press my own needs into the smallest corners,
tuck them beneath the weight of yours,
fold them so neatly they almost disappear.

I have become provider, protector, pillar—
the man you refuse to be.
I steady your storms,
hold the door open for your rage to pass through,
catch your moods before they hit the ground.

You flinch at the sight of your own reflection in me,
call me too much, too strong,
too there.
But you never seem to mind
that I am the one holding us together.

And still, when your silence falls heavy,
when you vanish into the comfort of your own indifference,
when I become nothing but a flicker at the edge of your vision,
you expect me to wait.

And I do.

Because I love you.
And I wish—God, I wish—
that you loved me the same.

Peanuts & Chlorine

You smelled like chlorine the first time you lied to me,
skin slick with the ghost of water,
eyes reflecting something too sharp to be light.

I tasted peanuts on your breath the last time you swore you cared,
salt clinging to the spaces between your teeth,
the aftertaste of something that should have been nourishing
but only choked me instead.

We were always treading water,
lungs half-full of the weight of it,
gripping at air that never wanted to hold us.

We were always cracking shells,
splitting things open to find nothing inside,
chewing on the remnants of what once was whole.

You smelled like chlorine the first time you lied to me.
I should have known then—
some things only seem clean until you get too close.

Hunger & Hands

You don't love me.
You love that I bend,
that I soften beneath your touch,
that I do not fight the shape you press me into.

You love the way I yield,
how easily I dissolve into the spaces you make for me,
how I never ask for room of my own.

You love the way I make you feel—
whole, wanted, unshaken.
You love the way I pour myself into you,
like water into cupped hands,
even as you let me slip through the cracks.

I am starving.
You are full.
And still, you hold out your hands for more.

Silent Scream

I want to scream,
but my throat is torn—
a hollow windpipe, frayed at the edges,
words catching like broken glass.

I open my mouth,
but only echoes spill out,
thin, unravelled, lost before they reach you.

You wouldn't hear me anyway.
You live where silence is comfortable,
where my suffering is background noise,
where my voice is nothing
but a whisper swallowed whole.

I want to scream,
but my throat is torn—
and maybe that was your plan all along.

The Trade of Unfairness

What have I done to deserve this?

You—
the one who has wandered through ruin,
left wreckage in your wake,
worn sin like second skin—
walk away unscathed.

And I—
the one who stayed good,
kept clean hands and a steady heart,
held faith like a candle in the wind—
am the one left burned.

Why is it that you got the best of me,
the softness, the devotion, the unshaken belief,
while I got the worst of you—
the silence, the cruelty, the half-hearted love
that never quite made it to me whole?

What kind of justice is this?
What kind of fate?

Or maybe this was never fate at all—
just another bad trade
where I gave, and you took,
and called it love.

Broken Thread

A twist,
and the pulse falters.
What once held steady now wavers,
a thread snapped under pressure,
tearing through a fabric that refuses to unravel.

The weight lingers,
an invisible stone pressed into skin
that no longer knows how to carry.
I move with a rhythm that doesn't belong,
the music muted,
the steps unsure.

Hands once sure now tremble,
fingers that once grasped
now reach into air
too thin to hold anything.

But it's never about the hands,
never about the thread or the weight—
it's the spaces between,
the quiet hum that fills them,
the places where nothing is
but everything still shifts.

And so I wait,
for a silence to settle,
for a break in the storm
that never quite passes.

Phantom Limbs

There is a room filled with echoes,
sentences unraveling at the seams,
syllables I stitched together in the shape of something soft,
something almost whole.
But nothing holds, not really—
not when touched by hands like yours.

I walk through the wreckage,
barefoot over remnants of what was nearly beautiful.
But beauty lingers—
and this was only ever fleeting,
a reflection in a window I mistook for an open door.

Maybe I was just staring too hard,
tracing constellations in static,
calling it fate.
Maybe I reached too far into a space
that was never meant to hold me.

But maybe won't rewind the reel.
Maybe won't unsplinter the bones.
Maybe won't make the silence taste any less bitter.
Maybe is just another kind of waiting, now.

Maybe, one day,
I'll wake up with lighter hands.
Maybe, one day,
the phantom ache will forget my name.

Somewhere Else

I dream of leaving.
I thought everyone did.
But people plant their feet so easily,
fold themselves into the same streets,
watch the same sun melt into the same earth,
and call it enough.

I listen for the restless hum beneath their words,
some small tremor of elsewhere,
but all I hear is stillness—
a kind of comfort I do not recognise.

For the Ones Who Go

You are for the dreamers,
the leavers,
the ones with untied laces
and maps folded wrong.

You speak in exit signs,
trace farewells into fogged-up glass,
watch the world from a window seat
and call it home.

Toxicology Report

I think I am poison—
not the kind that kills on contact,
but the kind that lingers,
that seeps into the roots of things
meant to bloom.

Everything good turns bitter in my hands.
Everything soft corrodes.
I watch joy flinch at my arrival,
watch love hesitate—
and I know.

I know.

The Space Between Us

I think I know someone.
I think we know each other—
almost too well, almost not enough.
I want us to fit like a secret,
to press into the shape of understanding,
but we keep our hands just shy of touching,
our words just short of meaning.

We orbit, we echo, we linger—
but never close the distance.

Unthoughts

Do you hate looking at me?
Do I unravel something in you
you'd rather keep stitched shut?

When our eyes meet across the room,
do you feel it—
the quiet devastation
of all that was never given the chance to ruin us?

Elissar Mustapha

Do you hate looking at me?
Do I unravel something in you

Unseen Shift

I don't remember when I started caring,
or when care turned into love—
it just happened,
slipped in unnoticed,
like the way a shadow falls without sound.

But now,
I would burn the world for you,
without question,
as if you've always belonged
to the list of things I'll guard
from the sharp edges of life.

Forbidden Fruit

The allure of the forbidden fruit—
I'll tell you what this means,
it's the pull of something so sweet
yet stitched with thorns,
the taste that lingers long after you've touched it,
the ache of wanting what was never meant to be had.

It's the quiet knowing
that desire wears a mask
and every bite leaves you
hollow but craving more.

The Weight of Now

Have you ever stood still,
looked down at your toes,
rooted into the earth beneath you,
and wondered—

What am I doing here?
What is my purpose?
Why?

The questions settle like dust,
quiet but suffocating,
and you feel the pull of something,
but it slips through your fingers
like the air you breathe.

The Ruin

You approached me with a machete in hand,
sliced into me with brutal precision,
and left a hole too wide to ever stitch.

I miss you
like a heart that once beat with heat,
now hollow,
frozen from the centre of my chest,
spreading across this distance
that eats us whole.

Every notification cuts deeper,
ghost of you that never really left.
Your absence lingers in the spaces between breaths,
in the silence where your name should be.

I was foolish to dream of forever
when we were already burning out
before we even learned to burn.

Now, I'm left with the remnants,
of what could've been,
fingers grasping for something that slipped through
like sand,
leaving only the ache of how we never learned
how to hold on.

Behind Opaque Glass

Do you want me to be nothing?
Nameless, faceless, voiceless—
buried behind a polished glass,
only to be seen when it serves you,
when it strokes your ego,
and satisfies your hunger.

You want me to disappear,
to be erased from the world
except when you call,
when you want me to please you,
a shadow you can summon
whenever it fits your need.

I'm nothing but a vessel for your pleasure,
a body to keep hidden,
to keep locked away,
and when you're done,
I vanish into the silence
where I was never meant to be.

Unspoke

You made me feel like I could talk to you about anything,
but it seems you only wanted to hear the good things.
Or for me to set myself before you,
raw and bleeding,
so you could feel good while you cleaned me up.

And if it comes to light
that you're the one who's making me ache?
If you're the reason my mind plays games
and my stomach is sick—
am I not allowed to bring it up?

Fuel to the Flame

I am on fire,
burning ablaze,
I thought you'd take my hand
when it got too much,
share the heat and pain.

If not, I thought,
just maybe—
you'd pass me that bucket of water,
put out the rage, soothe the agony.
I begged and I begged.

But it turns out you were carrying
a bucket of gasoline,
laughing at my naïveté,
dousing me while I was already on fire.

I was a fool from the beginning
to think that you,
standing so close to my burning heat,
meant you cared how I felt.

I wish my eyes and ears burned first,
so I would've never noticed you
to begin with.

Fated Collapse

Sometimes, the end is etched in the beginning,
whispered in the cracks of our first moments,
a truth we bury beneath the weight of hopeful smiles.
We dance around it,
clutching at the illusion of change,
pretending that we can rewrite the story.

But deep down, we know—
no matter how fiercely we wish for another way,
the outcome has already been sealed.
And we will ache,
forever reaching for a different ending,
while time drags us towards the inevitable collapse.

Grave of Hope

I want to sleep on it,
bury the feeling so deep,
let it take residence
in my mental graveyard.

But maybe I'm still holding out false hope,
because everything in me
whispers to wait it out,
as if time will heal the wound,
but what's the point?

It lingers,
rooted in the silence,
and no matter how I try to silence it,
it stays.
Maybe it was never meant to die at all.

Unseen

I don't feel like a person when I'm with you,
and I don't mean in the way
that I should feel light,
comfortable, and free,
transcendent in my own skin,
floating above the weight of everything.

No.
I don't feel like a person with you—
like you see me as something to possess,
a thing to own,
not a soul to understand.

To you, I cannot think,
I cannot be—
I am a whisper,
a thing that speaks nonsense,
a body you move at will,
placed where you want me,
when you need me,
looked at only in the moments
when you feel the weight of your own loneliness.

I am not a person to you.
I am an object,
a shadow you push around,
a reflection you avert when it's too painful
to face.
I cannot stand my ground
because you never see the ground I stand on.

The Echo

The mirror cracks beneath the weight
of what was never meant to be seen—
my reflection splits,
a fractured line that only deepens
the divide I never knew I had.

I search for the shape that fits,
the one that makes sense of
this quiet hunger,
this ache that has no name.
But you,
you only press further into the space,
widening what was once whole
until it is too wide to fill.

The air has become thicker,
like each breath I take
weighs more than my lungs can carry.
I have never known grief like this,
never known what it meant
to hold something close
and have it burn you alive
with the weight of its absence.

I thought the hurt would end
once I found the one
to make it stop—
but you taught me that love
can be a blade

disguised as a hand that pulls you under.
You taught me that to be close
can feel like drowning.

Still, when I think of walking away,
the thought clutches at my chest,
a quiet storm of something unnamed
that lingers,
long after the storm should have passed.
And I wonder—
why does it hurt so much
to untangle my fingers
from what was never meant to hold me?

Sugar Water

you like your coffee sweet,

and i drown mine in bitterness,

two opposite extremes

that never seem to meet

but somehow always touch.

you say you like things wrapped in ribbons,

pretty in their neatness,

while i long for them raw,

untouched by any hand but my own.

perhaps that's the question,

the one we're too scared to ask—

are we meant to be?

the ache of something unsettled

is all i know,

a quiet hum beneath my skin.

i can't tell if you love me,

but the silence presses louder

than any word we could speak.

and still,

i wait—

hoping for something i'm not sure will come.

a day passed,

and something shifted

in the spaces between us,

but i couldn't name it then—

just a flicker,

a spark.

another came,
and what was once gentle
grew sharp,
like something alive,
but left me broken,
wounded in the silence.
the days turned,
and the bloom i thought i'd nurtured
became a vine that strangled.
now, i wonder if i was ever meant
to touch this love at all,
or if i was always just a visitor
in its chaos.
i am blind when i am in love,
my hands trembling from the weight
of what i can't see,
of what i'm too afraid to feel.
and yet,
when i imagine letting you go,
the thought burns through me,
like a knife through sugar water.
how can something so sweet
turn so bitter?
i am soft,
i am fragile,
and i am in love with an angry man
who burns everything he touches,
but somehow,
i still hold on.

who, me?

do i leave traces,
carve my name into their skin,
or am i just the echo of their own desires?
am i something to see,
or just something to reflect upon—
their own image,
their own need for validation?

i wonder,
do you love me,
or do you love the way i mimic you?
have i bent myself into your likeness,
shaped like water to fit your hands,
or do i stand alone,
a thing untethered,
unseen,
waiting to be known for my own self?
maybe i'm just a mirror
and i can never see beyond what you show me.
and now,
i can't even tell if i'm holding the glass
or if it's holding me.

accidental beauty

beauty hides in the quietest places,
like the fading glow of a tower at twilight,
or the unspoken richness of a new flavour
\dancing on your tongue for the first time.
maybe that's how i found beauty in you—
in the unnoticed,
the subtle things that only reveal themselves
once you've touched them,
once you've let them touch you.

you were beautiful,
but not in the way that makes you easy to love—
no, your beauty was an accident,
a collision of light and shadow
that never quite made sense
until i was already tangled in it.
how could something so beautiful
become the source of such pain?
how can someone so radiant
be the one to burn me?

poison

you feed me poison,
to entertain my tongue,
flavours like poison ivy—
sweet and curling,
tangled in the folds of my mouth.
i mistake it for pleasure,
a fleeting moment of indulgence,
but it burns,
leaves behind a scar
i can't forget.

each taste is a promise,
woven in the bitterness
of your hands,
and i swallow it whole,
not knowing how deep the wound runs.
you offer it with a smile,
but it's the kind that betrays,
the kind that makes you forget
that poison never feels like poison
until it's too late.

in reference to doctor who–

i'm a lot like the doctor, i think.
i don't like endings—
they taste too final,
like burnt-out stars collapsing in on themselves.

my heart is vast and insatiable,
a never-ending void,
a black hole swallowing light,
devouring every touch, every word,
and still—
it is empty.

what am i to do with it?
let it wander, let it ache,
let it stretch across galaxies
until it forgets what it was looking for?
or let it shrink,
fold in on itself,
and become nothing at all?

story of why i hate myself

they call it idleness,
as if i choose to sink—
as if the weight pressing into my skin
is anything less than an anchor.

i scrub my teeth like i am unearthing something,
dragging bristles over gums
until they are raw, aching,
proof that i tried.
but effort looks different in dim light,
doesn't it?
it moves slower,
stumbles where others sprint.

perhaps you see it in the way i avoid mirrors,
or in the way i let my hands rest,
unpolished, unpainted, untouched,
as if colour would expose the decay underneath.

maybe it's the stairs—
how they stretch longer beneath my feet,
twisting, spiraling, laughing at my reluctance.
you say it's simple—
up, up, up—
but you don't hear the way they hum,
don't feel them tilt beneath three pills
and a body that no longer obeys.

one day, when the sky crumbles,
someone will ask me how i remain so still.
"*i don't,*" i'll murmur.
"*i simply do not move.*"
pray to my god?
paint my face?
would it make a difference
if i wore the mask of someone whole?

one day, when the sky crumbles,
someone will ask me how i remain so still.
"*i don't,*" i'll murmur.
"*i simply do not move.*"

fault lines

there is a tremor beneath my skin,
a quake that never quite breaks.
i press my hands against my chest,
waiting for the aftershock,
but nothing comes.

i think i was meant to shatter—
to crack open like thunder,
to spill like a river after the storm,
to *feel* in a way that proves i am alive.
but instead, i am a dam,
holding back a flood that never overflows.

i want to weep until my ribs ache,
to scream until my voice frays,
to punch the silence until it bruises,
but i am marble—
polished, cold, and unmoved.

and so i sit,
watching the world mistake my stillness for peace,
as if my bones are not splintering beneath it all.

connected

the threads that bind us—
are they woven in fibre optics,
stitched together by wi-fi signals and fleeting pixels?
are we just echoes in an endless scroll,
names without weight,
faces without touch?

or do we exist in the spaces between—
in laughter shared over coffee-stained tables,
in a knowing glance across a crowded room,
in the hush of a late-night call,
where words mean more than their syllables?

maybe connection is both—
a whispered joke between strangers on an escalator,
a glance at flashing lights once thought decoration,
a phrase half-heard, half-understood,
but somehow, completely felt.

"*you can wait*"
—an anthem for the eldest daughter

you can wait—

when the little ones cry,

when the world pulls you apart at the seams,

when your hunger gnaws like an echo in an empty room,

but their plates must be filled first.

you can wait—

when your hands ache for softness,

for warmth that isn't borrowed,

for love that isn't duty-bound.

you can wait, because you always have.

you can wait—

when your dreams sit untouched,

gathering dust beside childhood diaries,

because there is always something more pressing,

something heavier, something not yours

but carried anyway.

you can wait—

and maybe someday,

someone will tell you,

"*you don't have to.*"

encapsulate

i wish i could bottle my pain,
press it into something small, something digestible,
a pill you could take with your morning coffee,
let it dissolve on your tongue, seep into your
bloodstream,
so you'd finally understand—

the way it lingers, heavy and bitter,
the way it claws at my ribs, relentless,
the way it never quite leaves,
only settles deeper,
only becomes part of me.

i wish you could swallow it whole,
feel it tighten around your throat,
turn your stomach inside out,
make you taste the way i ache—
so maybe, just maybe,
you wouldn't call it imaginary.

stoneheart

ignorance stretches across the nation,

a creeping vine of distrust,

this society, my birthplace,

where i was raised,

where i thought i could belong,

now suffocates me with its demands.

they attack without understanding—

my religion is not a weapon,

it is a plea for peace,

a prayer for unity.

this is my home,

yet they don't see it.

opinions of islam are rotting in the past,

frozen in time like a broken mirror,

unable to reflect what is true.

brittle judgments,

ignoring the beauty beneath,

demanding answers that don't exist.

ignorance spreads like wildfire,

fueled by fear,

burning through the roots of our society,

leaving ashes where understanding should be.

in this land, corruption festers,

hidden beneath the surface of polite conversation,

infecting the minds that refuse to listen.

i was a child when i learned
people would hate me—
not for what i did,
but for who i was.
not because i was flawed,
but because my skin, my name,
my faith,
was painted with the brush of fear.

adults, living in bubbles of false comfort,
with hearts full of hate,
hoping for curses
for people they've never met,
never taken the time to understand.

"benefit of the doubt,"
that's what i was taught,
to offer even when the world withholds,
to trust when trust feels like a broken promise,
because who knows—
maybe one act of kindness
could crack the stone around a heart
buried in hatred.

the art of leaving

i cup my hands beneath a leaking faucet,
watching the water spill through the cracks of my fingers,
watching love slip the same way—
never held, never whole.

i swallow goodbyes like bitter pills,
each one catching in my throat,
each one shaped like the sound of my own name
when spoken by a mouth that never learned to love me gently.

i fold myself into an envelope,
seal my ribs shut with trembling hands,
but i am always returned to sender—
unwanted, unopened.

somewhere, a house is burning.
somewhere, the match is still warm in my palm.
somewhere, i tell myself,
this is not loss. this is making room.

and yet—
i kneel at the altar of all that was,
press my forehead to the cold, hard truth,
and pray for the strength
to finally walk away.

a slow unbecoming

i peel myself off the walls,
dust where a portrait used to be,
where hands once framed me in gold,
where silence now curls its fingers around my throat.

a bird learns the weight of its own wings
only when the cage door yawns open—
only when the sky is too wide, too empty,
too much like a question with no answer.

i chew on echoes,
spit out the vowels of a name i no longer recognise,
watch them pool at my feet,
spilled ink, spoiled milk, something once soft now curdled.

there is a house with my shape carved into its doorframe,
a window that still holds my breath on cold mornings,
but when i knock,
the stranger inside wears my face and does not let me in.

i think i used to belong here.
i think i used to be whole.
i think i will never know which loss came first—
the leaving, or the love.

Elissar Mustapha

the undoing

you should have warned me—
that love tastes like salt in an open wound,
that it burrows beneath the ribs,
a parasite with hands too familiar,
a ghost with my name in its throat.

i am unthreading myself from your touch,
pulling apart each stitch you wove into my skin,
but you were meticulous, weren't you?
tangled me into your breath,
sewed me into your silence,
left me unraveling at the seams.

if i could cut the cord clean,
if i could walk away without the weight,
if i could forget how your voice once
fit against the soft of my ear—
but i was built to remember.

so i claw, i tear, i scrape.
i try to make a home inside the empty,
but your echo is still in the walls,
and my hands
are still bleeding.

toward the sun, still

we were born in the wreckage,
spat out by the teeth of the storm,
hands calloused before they ever held softness.

the road was never paved—
only dust and longing,
only footsteps sinking into yesterday's ghosts.

but we carve, we build, we bleed—
we shape tomorrows out of ruin,
stack our dreams like bricks
even as the wind howls them down.

the night is long,
the sky is heavy,
but we are relentless—
two silhouettes against the dark,
digging, climbing, burning,
until the sun knows our names.

cracked pepper water cracker

a brittle edge,
sharp and delicate
like the first taste of silence
between two old friends—
no words, just the crackle,
just the bite.

thin as the lies we tell ourselves,
yet sharp as the truth we swallow
when the night is quiet.

soft, but not tender.
cracked pepper, but nothing to numb the burn.

we break,
we crumble,
we crunch
under the weight of something too small to hold.

still,
we carry it,
one more nibble of the impossible.

Elissar Mustapha

drowning in dryness

i swallowed the sun,
but it never warmed my throat.
a dry river in the cracks of my chest,
parched under skies that refused to rain.

you carved your name in dust,
and i inhaled it—
a slow death that tasted like glass,
sharp and cold,
burning my lungs with every breath
i wasn't allowed to exhale.

i used to dream of drowning—
of water,
of drowning in the soft weight of you,
but all i have is this
thirst
that never dies.

a breathless ocean in my chest,
a tide that's lost its rhythm,
waving for something
that doesn't come.
i ache in silence
for a rainstorm
that never touches me.

hands reach,
but they crumble in the wind—
sand slipping between my fingers
as i grasp for the echoes
of a life that never made it
past the horizon.

you burned me with your absence,
and i learned to drink dust
instead of air.
the flames keep licking at my skin,
but there's no moisture left
to put out the fire.

i am an echo now,
a shadow of something
that once lived,
drowning in dryness,
fading in the stillness
of a world that forgot to breathe.

and i wait—
wait for something to fill
the hollow in my bones,
but all i taste is dust,
and it never quenches.

the man who unmade me

i leave,
but my shadow stays.
it lingers where your voice still lives,
in the spaces between ribs you caged me in,
in the cracks you carved into my softness.

you were my solace,
but never my safety.
you were the fire,
and somehow the only warmth i knew.
you were the wound,
and the only hands i let stitch me back together,
over and over,
until my body was nothing but scar tissue
shaped like your name.

how cruel,
to run from the knife
but long for the hand that held it.
to beg for mercy from the mouth
that only ever learnt to hurt me.
to whisper,
i love you
when all you've ever done
is teach me how to survive pain.

you say you've changed.
soft words, spun from regret,
woven from guilt i never asked to hold.

love bomb detonating in my chest.
i know this script.
i have memorised the rise and fall of your remorse,
the way your voice cracks just enough to make me stay.
but i also know what comes after.

if i leave, i lose you.
if i stay, i lose me.
tell me,
which is the greater tragedy?

and yet,
here i am, hands shaking,
mourning what will never be—
the laughter we never reached,
the life we never built,
the future i kept trying to write,
as if love alone could force your hands
to be anything but cruel.

i will break my own heart
before i let you break me again.
i have to.
because the only thing worse
than losing you,
is losing myself
one more time.

when love feels like leaving a grave

i tell myself, this time, i will leave.
i whisper it like a prayer,
like a hymn,
like an exorcism.
i fold it into the corners of my mouth,
taste the salt of it on my tongue.
but then your voice crawls through the cracks,
soft, repentant, sweet as poisoned fruit.
you are sorry.
you have changed.
you will never hurt me again.

and my ribs, fragile things,
remember the shape of your love
before they remember the bruises.
my hands, traitorous hands,
ache to trace your jaw
before they recall how they once covered my ears
to block out the shouting.
my mind, foolish, aching, desperate,
claws through the wreckage
for any memory that doesn't burn.

i tell myself, *this time, i will leave.*
but the moment i reach for the door,
grief splits me open like a wound unhealed.
what about his birthday gift?
the one i spent months curating,

love woven into every detail?
what about the first snowfall i wanted us to see together?
the city we dreamt of moving to?
the life i imagined,
the life i begged for,
the life i will never get to hold?
what happens to all the versions of us
that only existed in my head?

i mourn them.
i mourn them like the dead.
i mourn them as if they were ever real,
as if they weren't just my own hands
grasping at straws,
trying to build a home in a house set aflame.

you were my lover.
you were my best friend.
you were the man who hollowed me out
and called it devotion.
and yet, when the world turns cold,
why is it your arms i want to crawl into?
why does the source of my pain
feel like the only place i can find relief ?

this is what you have done to me.
this is what loving you has made of me.

but i know how this ends.
the cycle, the breaking, the mending,
the soft apologies wrapped around hidden knives.

i know what happens when you feel safe in my forgiveness.
i know what happens when you stop being afraid to lose me.
i know, and i still hesitate.
god, why do i still hesitate?

perhaps because leaving you
feels like tearing a limb from my body.
perhaps because i do not know
who i am without your hands holding me in place.
perhaps because i have lived so long
shaped by your love
that i am afraid to meet the girl
who will stand in the mirror without you.

but i have to.
because if i stay,
there will be nothing left of her to find.

ghost of a girl

i tell myself i hate you.
let the words settle on my tongue,
dry and unfamiliar, like an ill-fitting lie.
i try to wear them anyway,
but they slip right off,
pool at my feet,
make a fool of me.

i do not hate you.
i wish i did.

hate would be easier than this,
this endless ache,
this war between knowing and feeling,
between the truth and the way my hands still shake
when they reach for you in the dark.

you are my deepest wound,
and yet i press my fingers to you,
again and again,
like i am searching for a pulse.
as if something inside me still believes
you are where i come alive.

but what life is this?
what life have i carved from your love?
i am not a woman anymore—
just a collection of compromises,
of silences,

of things i have swallowed whole
to keep the peace.
to keep *you.*

you say you've changed.
you kiss me gently,
the way i once begged you to.
you lace your fingers through mine,
whisper my name like a vow,
and i want to believe it,
i want to drink down this moment
like it is holy,
like it is something more than
another trick of the light.

but i know you.
i know the way your promises wilt.
i know how your kindness is always on a timer.
and yet—god, and yet—
why does it still hurt to leave?

i think of the nights i spent dreaming of you,
of the girl i used to be,
the one who thought love meant sacrifice,
the one who thought she was strong enough
to be your softness.
i think of the future i built in my head,
where you are kind, where i am safe,
where none of this ever happened.

and i grieve her.
i grieve her as i would a ghost.
because that future does not exist.
because i cannot love you into being a better man.

because i cannot love you and survive.

but still, i stay.
still, i linger at the edge of this ending,
fingers curled around the life i should have left behind.
still, i let you pull me back,
one last time,
one last time,
one last time.

a death that never comes

just one more night,
or maybe the ghost of one.
one more hour folded into your arms,
cradling the ache like a newborn grief.
one more moment where i lie to myself,
where i let you lie to me too.

i tell myself this is the last.
but last times don't feel like this—
don't feel like hands that linger,
like breath held between teeth,
like drowning with lungs still full.

i want to be done with you,
with the ruin of us,
with the soft decay of what was.
but i also want to memorise you
so well that i never need to let go.

one last embrace,
one last time i press myself into you,
as if i could stitch myself into your skin,
as if i haven't already bled into every part of you.

but the mind is cruel and the heart is crueler,
and they play a game of war inside me.
one side begs me to run,
the other reaches for you
even as you unravel me thread by thread.

and when the night ends,
when the silence stretches,
i find myself whispering again—
just one more.
because the last time
never feels like the last.
because you are not a person,
you are a slow death,
and i am still waiting to die.

Elissar Mustapha

requiem for the girl i was

i found her body in the wreckage,
a girl i used to know—
bright-eyed, full of fire,
laughter strung between her teeth like pearls.
she was golden once,
spun from something fearless,
something that did not beg to be loved.

i remember her.
she had hands that reached for the world,
a voice that did not tremble,
a spine unbent by the weight of a name
that was never meant to be carved into her ribs.

but then,
you.

you, with your promises
like honey laced with glass,
with your hands that held only to hollow,
with your love that felt like a funeral
i wasn't meant to walk away from.

you took her.
you drained the light from her lungs,
whittled her down to silence,
stitched your name into her skin
until she forgot how to answer to her own.

and now—
now i sit in the empty shell of her body,
wearing her ghost like a poorly fitted dress,
wondering if she ever really existed
or if she was just a dream
i was never meant to wake from.

...

your hands,
slick with promises that rotted in the air,
peeled me apart, layer by layer,
until all that was left
was the hollow sound of my own breath
against the walls of a body i no longer recognise.

i have not seen her in so long.
the girl who laughed without looking over her
shoulder,
who spoke without trembling,
who took up space and thought it was her right.
i think you killed her.
i think i let you.

and now,
i sit among the ruins,
sifting through dust,
searching for pieces of a past life
that will never fit this body again.

what a cruel trick,
to love the hands that built my grave.

requiem for the taste of you

you melt on my tongue like rosemary crackers,
a quiet crumble of something once whole,
something savoury, something fleeting,
the aftertaste lingers long after the bite.

i close my mouth around the memory,
but it dissolves too quickly,
a ghost of warmth, a whisper of salt,
you were always slipping through my teeth.

i tell myself not to reach for more,
but hunger is cruel, and habit is hungrier,
so i trace the flavour back to your hands,
to the way you once pressed life into mine.

i do not crave you,
only the taste of what was,
only the scent of rosemary on your fingertips,
only the echo of something i can never swallow whole again.

requiem for my own damn mercy

i am an inferno swallowing itself whole,
a fire too polite to burn the house down,
i should be an earthquake, a tidal wave, a reckoning—
but instead, i am a girl who stays.

you do not see my worth,
and maybe that is my greatest sin,
not that you are blind,
but that i let you close your eyes.

i let you carve me into something smaller,
let you fold me into something softer,
let you carry me like a weightless thing
when i was never meant to be weightless.

you have broken me in ways i cannot count,
and yet my hands still shake at the thought of leaving.

what kind of sickness is this?
what kind of love?

i should be enough to myself.
i should be enough to myself.
i should be enough to myself.

but still, i stay.
still, i wait.
still, i pray for the day you look at me
and see what i have bled to prove.

and god, i hate myself for it.

the taste of you

you are a pomegranate piece,
a glistening promise between my teeth,
all sweet flesh and crimson lure,
but it is only ever the surface—
thin, fleeting, a deception of depth.

the deeper i go,
the faster i hit the truth,
a bitter pit masquerading as something whole,
something worth keeping.
you are a thing that wounds the tongue
when held too long,
a thing that refuses to be swallowed.

but still, i bite down.
still, i let the bitterness coat my mouth,
as if i do not know
how this always ends.

hushed

it does not gnaw today.
does not pull, does not beg.
the air is still, the light is soft,
and the green spreads like quiet surrender
over something once too brittle to hold.

the first bite—
not desperation, not prayer,
just warmth against the roof of my mouth,
just something soft, something whole.

no ache, no longing,
only the slow dissolve
of what was withheld,
only the quiet knowing
that hunger, too,
can learn to rest.

the slow-earned ruin of me

it comes like dusk,
slow and unrelenting,
the weight of too many nights spent
bargaining with ghosts.

i peel myself off the mattress
like old wallpaper,
fragile, flaking at the edges,
aching in places i can't name.

what does rest taste like
when sleep is war?
when even silence hums
with the echo of something i lost?

i have carried too much,
loved too hard,
bled too quietly—
and now, i am spent,
spooled out like thread
too thin to weave into anything new.

god, if you love me,
let me disappear
just for a little while.

let me be
somewhere quiet,
somewhere far,
somewhere i do not have to be
anything at all.

no one warns you how good the fall feels

it starts like a whisper.
like a hand on my back that isn't mine.
like a gentle nudge towards the abyss—
just to see, just to peer over the edge.
just to feel something new.

and god, do i feel it.

at first, it's light, it's air, it's weightlessness.
it's standing on a rooftop at midnight
with the wind in my lungs and the city lights below
whispering *jump* just to see if i can fly.

but then—then it becomes something else.
the air gets thinner,
the ground gets closer,
and suddenly i'm clawing at nothing,
grasping at walls that aren't there,
begging for a hand that i swore i didn't need.

but there is no hand.
just the fall.

just the sick thrill of knowing
i did this to myself.
i let the rot creep in,
i let the fire spread,
i let him carve my name into his teeth
until i forgot how to say it myself.

and oh, how i *loved* the carving.
how i let him hollow me out,
scoop the insides,
fill me with his name,
his wants,
his rage,
his silence,
until i wasn't even a person anymore—
just a shell of what he needed.
a marionette with pretty strings.
but marionettes don't scream.
and i—i am screaming.

screaming in the grocery store when i reach for something i
used to love,
screaming in the mirror at a face i barely know,
screaming when i hold my own hands and wonder
when did they stop feeling like mine?

i spiral, i scream, i crash.

and the worst part?
i still miss the fall.

the stain of you

you split open like a pomegranate,
red spilling from your mouth,
from your hands, from the wounds
you swore you didn't leave.

i press my lips to the promise of sweetness,
but it is a thin disguise,
a fragile veil over the hard truth of you—
the bitter pit at your core.

you stain everything you touch.
your "love" seeps into my skin,
a red i cannot scrub away,
no matter how many times i try,
no matter how raw my hands become.

and still, i reach for you.
still, i taste the ruin of you,
as if i do not know
that red only ever means bleeding.

the slow-earned ruin of me

it comes like dusk,
slow and unrelenting,
the weight of too many nights spent
bargaining with ghosts.

i peel myself off the mattress
like old wallpaper,
fragile, flaking at the edges,
aching in places i can't name.

what does rest taste like
when sleep is war?
when even silence hums
with the echo of something i lost?

i have carried too much,
loved too hard,
bled too quietly—
and now, i am spent,
spooled out like thread
too thin to weave into anything new.

god, if you love me,
let me disappear
just for a little while.

let me be
somewhere quiet,
somewhere far,
somewhere i do not have to be
anything at all.

Elissar Mustapha

no one warns you how good the fall feels

it starts like a whisper.
like a hand on my back that isn't mine.
like a gentle nudge towards the abyss—
just to see, just to peer over the edge.
just to feel something new.

and god, do i feel it.

at first, it's light, it's air, it's weightlessness.
it's standing on a rooftop at midnight
with the wind in my lungs and the city lights below
whispering *jump* just to see if i can fly.

but then—then it becomes something else.
the air gets thinner,
the ground gets closer,
and suddenly i'm clawing at nothing,
grasping at walls that aren't there,
begging for a hand that i swore i didn't need.

but there is no hand.
just the fall.

just the sick thrill of knowing
i did this to myself.
i let the rot creep in,
i let the fire spread,
i let him carve my name into his teeth
until i forgot how to say it myself.

and oh, how i loved the carving.
how i let him hollow me out,
scoop the insides,
fill me with his name,
his wants,
his rage,
his silence,
until i wasn't even a person anymore—
just a shell of what he needed.
a marionette with pretty strings.

but marionettes don't scream.
and i—i am screaming.

screaming in the grocery store when i reach for something i
used to love,
screaming in the mirror at a face i barely know,
screaming when i hold my own hands and wonder
when did they stop feeling like mine?

i spiral, i scream, i crash.

and the worst part?
i still miss the fall.

no one sees the quiet

the walls are soft with rot—
not enough to fall,
just enough to breathe mould.

mornings taste like metal and sickness,
nights like burnt wick.
i light a candle
just to watch it drown in its own wax.

i love with a question
pressed beneath my tongue.
he says forever
like it's a magic trick.
once, he disappeared.
i clapped anyway.

my mother prays
in rooms i'm not allowed in,
for a version of me
that never loved him.

i lace the ring like armour—
tight enough to bruise,
loose enough to lose.
some days i forget it's there
until my finger throbs with wear.

i'm 22
but i wait to be called
before i speak.

i peel decisions off the skin
like labels
and apologise
for the way i breathe.

there's a mirror i avoid—
it flinches first.

i don't go home.
the doorknob stares.
the bed speaks in static.
every object asks
where i've been.

i stay inside my body
like a locked room—
curtains drawn,
breath folded small,
hoping no one knocks.

but silence
stretches its mouth too wide
and loneliness
sits cross-legged on my chest
and asks if i remember
what being held feels like.

i don't.

i only know
how to cradle weight
until my bones forget
they weren't born for this.

Elissar Mustapha

i'm so tired of being alive like this

there's a fog inside my ribs that never clears—
just hangs like a half-spoken sentence,
choking every breath that tries to finish.

i plant good intentions like glass seeds,
but they bloom into cuts—every step forward
carves another apology into my ankles.

he holds me
like a man who never dropped me,
but i still feel the crack from when he did.
some ghosts only live in touch.

i keep wondering if we're real
or just desperate.
we paint over cracks in the same old wall
and call it a new home.

my mother speaks in detonations.
every silence between us
ticks.
she wants me somewhere far from what i chose.
but love isn't always the safest thing.
sometimes, it's a fire escape
we mistake for a staircase.

i don't have a job,
but i wake up exhausted.
don't have a voice
but my throat stays sore

from swallowing every scream
that says
please let me be mine.

i walk past mirrors like
they owe me something and never pay up.
i dress in vanishing.
i smile like a glitch.

i don't want to be perceived,
but loneliness has claws.
and i sleep
with its hands around my throat.
there's a version of me buried under all this weight—
she used to sing in the shower,
used to think the future
was a bright thing.

now
i just want one day without the static.
one breath without the burn.
one night where my heart isn't a hostage
tied to a love
i keep trying to rescue
from the fire
it lit.

but i love him.

they all say
get the hell out.
every last one.
sister, friend, ghost, God—
they look at me with mourning in their eyes
like i've already died.

i nod.
i agree.
i know he's no good for me.

but then
his name slips past my teeth
like a confession i can't choke down.
my mouth forgets how to lie
when it's full of his name.

they say this is killing me.
but how do i explain
i've already built a coffin with my own hands,
lined it in all the times he almost changed.

i keep saying
he's trying,
and they keep saying
you're drowning.

but i swear, some nights he loves me so quiet,
so almost-right, it hurts less than usual.
and that's something, isn't it?

he makes a mess
then offers a broom
and i call it growth.
they say
that's not healing—
that's hell with flowers.
but i'm still here,
chained to the hope
that maybe this time
he won't set the match.

i don't know what's wrong with me.
why love tastes like ash
and i still lick the plate clean.
they scream
leave
like it's a switch i haven't found,
but my legs forgot how to run
the day he said
you're overreacting
and i believed it.
they don't see
how soft he becomes
when i beg.

they don't know
what it's like
to be goddamn haunted
by someone who holds you
like a prayer and a punishment
in the same breath.

and maybe i do deserve more.
but he's what i want.

and i hate that.
and i love that.

and i don't know
if that makes me loyal or lost.

or just another girl
too in love with the fire
to crawl out of it.

what now?

how am i supposed to survive this?
no, really—
how do i keep breathing
with his name
still splintered in my throat?

how do you stitch up a wound
that's been rewounded so many times
it forgot how to close?

what am i even supposed to do?
everyone keeps saying
you'll be okay
like that means a damn thing
when the nights keep opening their jaws around me.

i didn't ask for this.
i didn't want this.

i wanted love, not a war inside my chest.
so why me?
why this?
why him?
why give me a love that feels like drowning
with lungs that remember air?
i keep looking for instructions.
a manual.
a sign.

something that says:
here's how you get through heartbreak
when your heart still beats for the one
who broke it.
but all i get is silence.
and flashbacks.
and the ghost of his voice telling me it's my fault.

god,
what if i never get out?
what if this is the rest of me—waking up with my ribs caved in
and calling it morning?

i want to scream
but no one would understand the sound.
i want to run, but i'm still holding his hand in the back of my mind.
they say healing isn't linear—but no one said
it would feel like crawling through glass
just to remember who i was
before him.

what do i do?
what do i do?

someone, please—
just tell me how to let go
when every part of me is still
holding on.

i don't know who i am without him

i used to have edges.
a voice.
a name that felt like mine.

but now—i only know how to love him
in ways that cost me everything.

i shrink when he frowns.
i change when he's cold.
i apologise when he's tired
of holding the weight he gave me.
i don't know who i am without the ache of him inside me.

they say
you'll find yourself again,
but what if this is who i am now—
a girl with bruised hands from holding on too gently
to someone who never planned to stay?

what if the version of me before him was the dream
and this is the truth?

this isn't love, is it?

some nights i rehearse goodbye in my head
like a play i'll never perform.
i imagine myself walking away.

strong.
sure.
free.

but i always wake up still here.
still his.
still trying to make a bed out of broken glass
and calling it comfort.

this isn't love, is it?
it's grief with a heartbeat.
it's waiting for a man to stop hurting me
long enough to call it progress.
and maybe that's the cruelest part:
he doesn't even have to be cruel anymore.
i do it for him.

i hear the universe, but i'm still here

the signs are everywhere:
in the way my stomach knots when he texts me late,
in the way my friends go quiet whenever i say
but he's getting better.

the universe is screaming;
go.
run.
save yourself.

every door creaks like a warning.
every silence stretches like a prophecy.
every time i cry alone,
the world feels like it's trying to pry me out of his hands.

but still,
i stay.
i love.
i fight.

my heart doesn't listen to red flags.
it hears his voice and folds itself into forgiveness one more time.
i want to believe this can work.
i want to believe there's light under all this ash.
that maybe, if i just hold on tighter,
he'll remember how to be gentle with me.

i keep thinking maybe the universe is wrong.
maybe this pain is just the part before it gets good again.
maybe healing looks like holding on even when it hurts.

but deep down, i know you can't fix a burning house
by staying inside it.

and yet, here i am,
curled in the smoke,
calling it love,
telling the wind to hush as it pulls at my sleeves
like a mother saying,
please, come home.

sugar glass

of course it broke.
the jar—red like regret,
heavy with nothing but plans.
it slipped, like they all do eventually.

concrete is honest like that.

the splatter looked like something
sacred, or stupid.

(*i stood there too long,*
watching it bleed.)

no one teaches you what to do
when your day spills out
in aisle 3
of an open sky.

i licked syrup off my fingers earlier,
called it lunch.
called it survival.
called it
"i'm fine."

i am soft,
too soft,
a bruise that apologises when touched.
he is all corners and curses.
i mistake his storms for warmth.

i tell myself the lightning is just loud affection.
that silence is a kind of care.

(i have never been good
at not believing
in ghosts of things
that never loved me.)

maybe i see too much, read the cracks like scripture,
paint hearts on potholes.
maybe it was just tomato paste.
but it felt like a eulogy.
and that, i think,
is the problem.

swallow

there's a taste like coins at the back of my throat
a dull, metallic ache of words i don't say.
i bite them back until they rust,
until i forget what it felt like to speak without flinching.
you win.
you always do.
not because you're right
but because i let you.
because your silence weighs more than my pain.
i've learned how to fold, how to dim,
how to keep the peace by tearing little bits off myself.

you're more stubborn.
you dig in like roots, while i bend like wind.
and somehow i'm the one who apologises for the storm.

even when i bleed,
i soften.
even when i ache,
i hush.
i walk on eggshells like they're holy ground,
each crack a guilt i shouldn't carry
but do.
because all that matters is that you're okay.
and me?
i've swallowed so much of myself
there's hardly anything left to chew on.
just this sharp,
iron taste
of love gone wrong.

wake

the night's a thief stealing the quiet,
locking the door behind me— i'm left pacing
an empty room that hums with ghosts.

the bed is a cage of tangled thoughts,
and my own breath is the clink of chains
i didn't ask for.

i want to sleep,
but sleep wants no part of a mouth full of ash
and a heart carved out by hands that never rest.
the dark doesn't soothe; it sharpens,
turns my mind into a razor's edge
cutting over old wounds that still bleed secrets.

i'm a marionette with tangled strings,
dancing in the silence where mercy forgot to meet me.
and all the hours stretch like salt on an open cut—
no balm, no balm,
just the taste
of being wide awake
and utterly broken.

off track

everyone's moving—fast,
like rivers that already know
where they want to end up.

and here i am,
wading through mud
with words on my lips that won't catch fire,
feet sinking in the quiet
where ambition goes to lose its way.

i'm planting seeds in winter soil,
watching others bloom in the bright,
and wondering if i'll ever find a season that fits.

there's a voice inside—
soft but sharp—
telling me i'm late,
slow,
too tangled in my own hesitations to keep up.

but maybe being lost is just the map
rewriting itself beneath my hands,
and maybe the ache of falling behind
is the quiet before the climb.

or maybe it's just a dark road
with no signs and a stubborn heart
that's not ready to stop walking.

twin flames

we flicker, two candles in the same room,
leaning toward the silence between the gusts.
time folds itself like worn paper,
creases where we never touch,
edges sharp enough to cut the quiet
into a delicate ache.

your flame hums close,
but never warm enough to burn the cold away.
i trace the smoke,
a dance we never learned to hold
not quite right,
but never wrong enough to let go.

we are the echo of footsteps that follow but never meet,
a song hummed out of sync—
beautiful,
fractured,
always just out of reach.

limbo

stuck between breaths
not here, not there,
just a quiet nowhere
where even the walls hold their breath, waiting.
i'm pacing a thin line, swaying like a tightrope
under a sky that can't decide—leave, stay—
words spinning like leaves caught in a wind
that never lands, and every step feels like a question
with no answer. fear lingers—a shadow behind me,
whispering what ifs on repeat,
a broken record i can't switch off.
no map, no compass, just this slow bleed of time wasted
waiting for a sign that might never come. so i stay—
a ghost in the silence, haunted by maybe
and the weight of the wrong move.

circles

spinning round and round,
like a scratched record that won't let go of the same old sound,
a song stuck in the grooves of yesterday's mistakes.
time drips slow, a leaking tap that fills no cups,
just empties patience into thin air,
while clocks laugh behind their glass faces,
counting seconds that never move forward.
i'm chasing shadows in a hall of mirrors,
where every step is the same step,
and the exit fades into another beginning
a loop folding back on itself, like tired hands trying to hold onto
nothing. waste is a whisper
soft, relentless, telling me i'm nowhere, and nowhere is all i know
a place between moments, a breath held too long, a story
with no ending.
and still, the circle keeps turning, a cruel dance i can't leave, and i
keep walking
trying to find what's been lostin the loop, trying to break the spin
without breaking myself.
but maybe the circle is me
the weight and the wings, the fall and the flight,
the endless spin of wanting
and never arriving.

raw nerve

my face is a mask that's cracked at the seams
smirks and sighs colliding in a war zone
behind eyes that won't quit burning.

i'm drowning in the silence of things i can't say,
choking on the words
i bury deep
so they don't explode
and burn the whole damn world down.

rage is a poison
i sip slow
bitter fire that curls around my ribs,
but i swallow it anyway
because breaking is not an option.
this fog inside me
a mess of tangled thoughts,
half truths,
lies i tell myself just to keep breathing,
just to survive another damn day.
i'm raw, i'm ragged,
i'm everything i hide
when the lights are on
and the world's watching.

and god,
sometimes i just want to scream
until my voice shatters the quiet
that's killing me.

altar or exit

some nights i scroll through wedding rings
till my fingers ache
and others
i rehearse leaving
with no bag, no note, no trace.

i wear this love like skin that doesn't fit
but still bleeds when peeled.

he says *mine* and i try not to hear
forever like a trap door.

i want to end it fast,
like tearing a page.
but i also want to marry him
beneath a sky
my mother won't look at
and pretend
i've never been afraid of being owned.

i don't know how to tell the difference
between commitment and surrender.
between safety and silence.

he holds me like a question
i'm too scared to answer.
some days i feel found.
others
i feel buried.

i love him until it bruises.
i love him and wonder
if love is supposed to feel
like bracing for impact.

i see our future
and flinch.

he is the only place
i've ever wanted to stay
and the reason
i keep the door half open.

i keep swinging
between becoming his
and becoming a ghost.

and neither
feels like a way out.

i don't want to leave, i want it to change

i don't want to break up.
i want this version of us
to rot.
to slip quietly into the dirt
and never claw back out.

i want the silence to stop
screaming.
i want to stop apologising
for bleeding too loudly
when the cuts
aren't mine.

i still love you.
but not like this.
not with my hands shaking
every time i reach for peace.
not with my voice
stuck in my throat
like a guilty thing.

i want a love
that doesn't walk me
to the edge
just to watch me wobble.

i want us to begin again
without the ghosts
we fed too long.

without the versions of us
that mistook control
for care.

i want to want you
without fearing
what wanting will cost me.

this isn't goodbye.
not to you.
but to the shouting,
the swallowing,
the pretending this is enough.

let this love die
so something gentler can survive.

something
where i don't lose myself to keep you.

i keep thinking i want to leave you,
but the truth is—i just want this version of us to end,
this bitter, broken, barely-breathing thing
we keep dragging around
like a body we refuse to bury.

i don't want to walk away from you,
i want to walk away from the way i've been loving you,
with my hands clenched and my voice bitten down,
with every small need of mine
folded into something quieter
just to keep the peace
you never really offered me.

i want to be able to look at you
without remembering the days i cried for hours
and you just sat there,
tired of the noise,
tired of the version of me
your silence kept creating.

i want to stop fearing the way you love me
because love isn't supposed to feel
like proving myself
just to be allowed to stay.

and maybe you don't see it
but this has never been about not loving you enough
it's about not surviving the way this love asks me to shrink.

i want a relationship
where i can breathe without earning it,
where being soft isn't a risk
and saying how i feel
doesn't start a war.

i want to laugh with you
without checking if you're in the mood.
and not wonder what i've done wrong.
i want to make mistakes
without it being the end of the world,
without being made to feel
like loving me is work.

i still want you—but i want a version of you that knows how
to meet me in the middle,

not one that watches me burn
and says i started the fire.

i want this love to survive,
but not like this.
not in this sick, twisted, exhausting shape
that makes me question myself
every time i dare to want more.

so no;
i don't want to leave you.
but i do want to leave
this version of us
behind.

and if that means letting everything we've built
fall to the ground
just so we can rebuild it with gentler hands—
then so be it.

because i'm tired of wondering if it's me,
tired
of trying to hold my breath long enough
to make you happy.
i'm not asking for perfection—
i'm asking for a love
that doesn't rot me from the inside out.
and if you can't give me that,
then maybe i wasn't meant
to stay after all.

squeezed from the inside out

lately i feel like i'm being squeezed from the inside out,
like someone reached inside my chest
and started twisting
everything that ever made me soft
into something sharp.

i wake up heavy.
not tired—just full.
full of words i don't say,
fears i've folded into silence,
questions i'm too afraid to ask
because i already know the answers
and they're the kind that ruin things.

i still love you.
god, i do.
but loving you has started to feel
like carrying a glass of water through a hurricane
and calling it commitment.
i'm always bracing for the next spill,
the next crack,
the next *what did i do this time?*

it's not that i want out…
it's that i want *relief.*
i want love to feel like something i can rest in,
not a place where i hold my breath
waiting for the storm to pass
only to realise
the storm is the shape of us.

i want to feel safe again
in my own body,
in your presence,
in the kind of silence that doesn't hum with tension.
i want to stop walking on eggshells
barefoot
just to prove to you something you already know.

you ask what's wrong
and i lie.
because the truth is too big
and too old
and too close to breaking everything
we swore we were building.

but you know.
you have to know.
you've felt it too…
this slow tightening,
this ache that doesn't come from nowhere.

maybe we love each other
but built this thing
with the wrong blueprints.
maybe we learned love
from the wrong people
and now we're trying to unlearn
with shaking hands
and wounded hearts.

i don't want to leave.
i just want
whatever this is
to let go of me.

just for one second.
so i can breathe
without guilt clinging to my ribs.

so i can love you
without feeling
like i'm disappearing to do it.

jealous of the air

he's jealous of the bloody air i breathe
like even oxygen
is some other man
i shouldn't let too close.

his love wraps around my neck
like hands that forgot
when to let go.

i can't look
without explaining,
can't laugh
without punishment,
can't exist
without proof
that i still want him.

and i do.
i do.
but want was never meant to feel
like suffocation.

i hold my phone
like a loaded thing—
every buzz
a trigger.
every pause
a crime scene
i have to defend.

my smile has started twitching
like a habit i can't unlearn.

he says
he loves me too much.
as if that's the answer
to all the bruises
i've hidden inside my voice.

i used to be warm.
now i flinch at mirrors
and avoid sunlight
because he taught me
to fear being seen.

i want to love him
without apology.
without shrinking,
without dressing down
my own aliveness
to make him feel safe.

but he is jealous
of the bloody air i breathe
and i am running

out
of

breath.

love like a sentence

i have let him imprison me in the name of love.
built the bars myself— each one a compromise,
each lock a silence
i swallowed to keep him close.

he didn't have to chain me.
i sat still.
called it devotion.
called it patience.
called it love
even when it bruised.

i learned to disappear without leaving.
to fold myself
small enough
not to trigger his storms.

he said stay
and i mistook it
for care.
mistook control
for closeness.
mistook my own withering
for proof that love was working.

i dressed my fear up
in softness.
let him write the rules
with ink that stained
my skin.

i held my tongue
until it cracked.
apologised
for the noise my needs made.
made peace with being hollow
as long as he didn't leave.

but love
should never feel
like serving time.
and i've been counting
the days
by the weight in my chest.

still,
i look at him
and ache to believe it was real.
because if it wasn't…
what have i been dying for?

i made a home in the cell

the walls weren't there
when i walked in
just his hands,
his eyes,
a voice that knew how to close doors
without slamming them.

i laid the bricks myself.
one smile.
one silence.
one sorry
i didn't need to say.

the air thinned slowly.
not enough to panic,
just enough
to forget how breathing used to feel.

he loved me
in a language i wasn't fluent in
but i kept translating myself
until nothing sounded right.

somewhere along the way
my reflection stopped waving back.
just sat still
behind the glass.

i forgot what it meant
to move
without permission.
to be colour.
to laugh
with my whole mouth.

he never asked for a prisoner.
but he kept the key.

and i kept calling it
Home.

quiet thing with a pulse

i walk around like a closed wound
hoping no one notices the bleeding.
it's all internal
but it leaks
through the way i flinch at kindness,
the way i don't answer the phone.

he calls it love,
but it feels like a noose made of silk.
i smile through the suffocation,
call it comfort,
call it anything but what it is.

there's something growing inside me
not a scream
not a voice
just
pressure.
like a balloon tied inside my ribs
and someone keeps breathing into it
and breathing
and breathing.

i think if i don't cut it open
i might disappear.

and maybe that's the point.
to vanish
before anyone realises
i was cracking in plain sight.

i touch the old scars
like they're maps.
familiar routes
back to a place
i swore i'd never return.

i hate this version of me— the trembling, the silence,
the mirror i don't recognise.
but she's all i have tonight.
and she wants to go.
and she wants to stay.
and she wants
to be okay
so badly, she'd bleed for it.

i'm not asking to be fixed.
just seen.
just held
like a thing
with a pulse
and a reason.

anger grew in my mouth

there was a girl
who used to wait for the kettle to finish
before speaking.
she folded time
like laundry—
neatly, with both hands.

now my jaw locks at sunrise.
i grind hours between my teeth
and spit them out
half-chewed.

patience left me in the middle of a sentence.
i didn't notice
until i raised my voice
and no one flinched.

i used to hold things—
grief, guilt, small misunderstandings—
like bird bones.
now i crush first,
ask questions later.

he tells me
i've changed
like it's a crime
and not a consequence.

he forgets
how many rooms i've screamed into
without making a sound.
how long i've worn my tongue down
trying to say it's fine
in ways that wouldn't start a fire.

anger didn't come crashing in.
it crept.
it curled up in my throat
and called itself home.
it rewrote my face
when i wasn't looking.

i miss the version of me
who didn't twitch at shadows,
who didn't taste blood
after every conversation.

but that girl
believed she had time.

this one
knows better.

i don't recognise this fire

there's a heat inside me
that never cools.
a tight, red ache
that presses against my ribs
like it's trying to crawl out
or kill me on the way down.

i don't know when i became this—
a fuse,
a flare,
a room with no exits.
i scream through my teeth
without making a sound.

i used to be gentle.
i remember that.
she braided silence into something sacred,
waited for people to understand her
even when they didn't.

but somewhere along the timeline
she cracked.
too many small tears
in the same place
and now i can't even look at myself
without wanting to apologise
or disappear.

i don't know how to get back to her.
i don't know if she's still waiting
or if she walked off without me.

some days
i try to be soft again,
but it feels like lying.
like dressing a wound
that's still bleeding.

and the worst part—
the part i don't say aloud—
is that the fire hurts me
more than it burns anyone else.
i'm the one
left coughing up smoke
in empty rooms,
begging for air
like i didn't light the match myself.

i want to come home to myself.
but every hallway echoes,
and every mirror looks away.

i am dying from the inside,
but no one's buried me yet.

rooms i'll never own

i dream of silence
like it's a lover
who never showed.

four walls,
sunlight folding in soft across a floor
that hasn't heard my name screamed.
a room that doesn't tense when i exhale.
a space where i am not
a daughter, a fiancée, a disappointment,
just
a body
with no debt to anyone.

i want to leave without explaining.
eat toast at midnight in my own kitchen.
let the air touch my skin
without someone asking why.
i want to be alone
not because i hate people—
but because i forget who i am
when too many eyes are watching.

but i am stitched
to this house,
to this life,
to expectations that never asked
if i could carry them.

and so i stay—
in a room that's not mine
in a mind that's too crowded
with voices that aren't even mine
but live there louder than i do.

i water the fantasy of leaving
like a plant i can't plant.
watch it grow inside my chest
and wither
and bloom
and die again.

one day,
i whisper.
one day i'll wake
and the air will be mine
to breathe.

until then
i carry the weight
and call it home.

nothing ever left

i am 22,
brushing my teeth
in the mirror that once watched me
slip notes to death
under the bathroom door.

this room
still hums with the breath i held
at fourteen—
when even the curtains felt like spectators
and the ceiling pressed down like it had something to prove.

i repainted the walls.
i moved the bed.
but the air still remembers
how i curled in on myself,
wishing to vanish
like steam from a shower that never got hot enough.

the door still creaks the same.
the corners still whisper.
and every time i open the cupboard,
i see her—
that girl who counted down days
like prison time,
who thought silence
meant safety.
i grew up.
but not out.

i'm still here.
older,
quieter,
less surprised by the way sadness
settles in like mould.
i cover it
with lipstick and long sleeves
and keep telling people
i'm just tired.

no one tells you
that survival can feel like
re-suffocating
in the same air
that almost killed you once.

same address

there's a patch in the ceiling
where the paint curls
like it remembers.

the floorboards hum
in a language
i almost forgot how to fear.

i walk through this house
like a shadow that grew up
but never moved out.

every mirror is a photo
i didn't take,
each drawer a sigh i left
folded between pyjamas.

i try to sleep.
the bed breathes too loud.

outside,
someone's always mowing the grass.
inside,
the air stays still—
too still.
i open the window.
the same wind
comes in.

it's been eight years and the walls still call me
by the wrong name.

soft animal

there's something gnawing again—
behind the ribs,
beside the voice
that never quite learned how to beg.

i trace myself in steam
just to see if i disappear slower,
just to prove
i was here
before the glass cleared.

some days, the air bruises.
some days, it's the quiet
that bites.

i dream of rooms with no corners,
of mouths that open
only for song.
i dream of shedding
without apology.

and when i wake,
my name fits like
a sweater from another life.
loose in all the wrong places.
tight where i can't breathe.

i never said i was drowning.
i just stopped waving.

inheritance

i've worn so many hands
they fit like skin.
somewhere along the line,
i forgot
which voice was mine.

the days move me
like thread—
tugged through needles
i didn't choose,
stitched into versions
i never meant to wear.

they call it duty,
they call it love,
they call it *just the way things are.*
i call it
a slow unravelling
i wasn't allowed to notice.

sometimes, i envy the birds
that land on wires,
not knowing what power runs beneath
or who built the towers
they rest on.
they just leave
when the wind says so.

but i've stayed.
and stayed.
and stayed.

but i've stayed.
and stayed.
and stayed.

until even my silence
learned how to obey.

no one asked if i could breathe

i have spent so long contorting myself into palatable shapes, twisting bone and voice to fit into the spaces they carved for me before i ever had the chance to ask what i wanted; so long pretending that silence was strength, that obedience was love, that disappearing a little each day was what it meant to be *good*.

they taught me how to speak softly, how to fold my hunger into napkins under the table, how to smile when i wanted to scream, how to stitch up my rage in time for dinner, how to live in a house that never belonged to me, in a body that felt like a borrowed garment pinned too tightly at the seams.

i am 22 and somehow still 14 and somehow still 7, still asking for permission to breathe, to rest, to exist without apology; and i am tired in the kind of way that sleep can't touch, tired like a room that's been locked for years and forgotten, tired like dust on a windowsill that dreams of wind.

i feel like something wild is clawing at my ribs, trying to make space inside a cage that keeps shrinking, and the more i try to keep it in, the more it thrashes, the more it bleeds, the more it begs me to either set it free or kill it before it burns everything down from the inside out.

i don't want to hurt anyone.
i don't want to hurt myself.
but i can't keep swallowing this fire
just to keep everyone else warm.

i am not your daughter
if daughter means sacrifice.
i am not your future wife
if wife means silence.
i am not your good girl
if good means gone.

i am still here.
i am still burning.
and one day,
i won't ask for the key—
i'll break the damn door.

lemon trees and nail polish 2

the lemon trees whisper in a language i can't unlearn,
their bitter fruit spilling like secrets into the soft pool of nail
polish drying on my skin—
a silent war between sharp edges and glossy masks,
while the cursed phone hums with a pulse that doesn't belong to me,
each vibration a ghost sliding beneath my ribs,
slipping between the cracks where my breath should be.

sweetness lingers—poisoned and patient—
wrapping itself around my throat like smoke from a fire that
never needed to start,
and i am both the ruin left behind and the one trying to sweep
the ashes,
hands raw and trembling,
chasing shadows that refuse to settle,
tasting bitter tea in every heartbeat,
an anchor dragging me under
to a place where past and future bleed
into the same slow ache.

here,
the present is a glass house filled with broken reflections,
and i am lost in the echoes—
not sure if i am the sound or the silence,
the wound or the healing,
the mess that needs mending
or the hands that can't stop breaking.

wet lacquer

the weight of wet lacquer clings like a secret i haven't
dared to speak,
each finger a breath held too long,
hovering over the edge of everything i want to touch
but cannot—
the world soft beneath my nails but too fragile for me to trust,
a thin glass membrane stretched between skin and air,
quivering with the threat of ruin
at the slightest careless brush or careless word,
and i am suspended
in the pause between beginning and break,
where silence tastes like waiting,
and hope is the trembling surface of something new
that could shatter
or harden
but not yet.

pressure system

i wasn't always this storm,
but now i hum with the sound of bursting—
the windows rattle when i breathe,
and there's glass behind my ribs
that keeps trying to break its way out.

i wake with clenched teeth
and sleep with fists that forget to loosen,
my voice echoing in my throat
like it's rehearsing a scream
that never gets born.

everything touches me too loudly—
the kettle boiling,
his silence on the phone,
the way the walls don't move
no matter how hard i push.

somewhere beneath all this red
was a quiet girl who knew how to wait,
but now even my shadow flinches
when i walk into a room,
and the mirror looks away first.

i hate the burn
but i don't know how to cool it,
don't know how to stop the tremble
that keeps climbing my bones,
don't know how to hold myself
without choking.

it feels like i'm one more breath
from combustion,
and no one taught me
how to be fire
without becoming ash.

i didn't mean to, but i did

i don't know when i started speaking like that—
sharp-edged and too fast,
like the words have waited years just to be ugly.
they tumble out now without permission,
and i hear myself mid-sentence,
but it's like trying to stop an avalanche
with bare hands and regret.

i used to be softer.
i used to press my tongue to the roof of my mouth
just to keep it all in,
all that heat, all that ache.
i used to be someone people liked.
i think i liked her too.

but lately,
i feel like i'm being stretched thin from the inside,
something too loud buzzing beneath my ribs—
like my lungs are going to shatter
if i don't scream.
and maybe i've already started,
not with volume,
but with the things i say now,
reckless,
like i want to ruin the room
just to prove that i'm still in it.

and it's not even about him.
not just him.
it's the years, it's the corners i sat in,
it's the no's i swallowed
because i was scared of what happens
when a girl says no too many times.

i hate who i'm becoming.
she's angry, she's bitter,
she bites first,
and she's always tired.
but i don't know how to get back
to the girl who forgave everything,
who smiled when she wanted to cry,
who whispered her feelings
so no one would be inconvenienced.

that girl doesn't fit anymore.
and this one's on fire.

and no, i don't know how to put her out.

Untitled

i watch the room catch fire
with something i didn't mean
but somehow always meant.

i used to measure myself
in teaspoons of restraint,
but now my hands shake too hard
to hold anything that small,
and the calm i wore like perfume
has soured into something heavier,
something that stings the skin.

i keep trying to swallow the rage
but it climbs, stubborn,
spilling out through cracks
i didn't realise were there—
cracks shaped like his name,
like the hours i've lost
folding myself into softer versions
so i wouldn't be too loud to love.

they think i'm too much
but don't see the weight i've carried
just to speak at all,
don't see the bruises on my silence,
don't know how it feels
to drown in words
you were never allowed to say.

and so it pours—
ugly, true,
the kind of truth that makes people flinch,
the kind of anger that doesn't ask permission,
the kind that burns through apologies
and still wants more.